M000035495

Walking in the Reign

30 Reflections from Seeking God's Will

By Lori Altebaumer and Emily Dehm

All rights reserved. Except for brief excerpts for review purposes, no part of this book may be reproduced or used in any form without written permission from the publisher.

Unless otherwise noted, all Scripture quotations are taken from the Holy Bible, New International Version®, NIV®. Copyright © 1973, 1978, 1984 by International Bible Society. Used by permission of Zondervan. All rights reserved. Scripture quotations marked NKJV are taken from the New King James Version®. Copyright © 1982 by Thomas Nelson. Used by permission. All rights reserved.

Copyright © 2020 Lori Altebaumer

Print ISBN: 978-0-578-63428

Praise for *Walking in the Reign*

There is truth all around us, if you take time to look. Lori Altebaumer has. She has found God in everyday places and experiences. The perception and depth of what she shares will transform the ordinary world around you into an instruction manual for your journey with Him. You will be inspired and encouraged after just a few minutes in this book. I loved it!

Julie Zine Coleman, Author of Unexpected Love: God's Heart Revealed through Jesus' Conversations with Women and managing editor for Arise Daily Devotionals

This beautiful collection of devotions clearly expresses the author's heart for the will of God and encourages readers to have the same. I enjoy how Lori connects the everyday to the Divine in these soothingly poetic yet spiritually challenging reflections. I recommend Walk in the Reign as I believe the devotions- many inspired by the author's travels- will benefit readers on their spiritual journey.

Heather Norman Smith, Author of Where I Was Planted and Grace & Lavender

Walking in the Reign is laced with just the right amount of humor and personal experience. I found myself smiling both with laughter and in wonder as I read these devotions. The words on the page came alive and took me to the places and through the experiences the authors have had. I learned so much and was reminded of so much in my own walk with the Lord through their words. The reflection questions aren't just a nice exercise. They cause real introspection and examination of the heart. Lori and Emily shared deep hearts in their own pursuit of God's will and encouraged me to do the same.

Donna Nabors, Author of Pearls: 5 Essentials for a Richer Prayer Life

In Memory of
Sandy Bills Steele

Who faithfully walked in His reign as a light to all who follow.

Walking in the Reign

Contents

Part I: Loving God

Part II: Loving Others

Part III: Loving Myself

Introduction

For since the creation of the world His invisible attributes are clearly seen, being understood by the things that are made, even His eternal power and Godhead, so that they are without excuse… (Romans 1:20).

Welcome to Walking in the Reign. There is a running joke in our family that if my husband plans a hiking trip and invites you along, you better bring a rain jacket. We fully expect, no matter what the forecast, that we will be walking in the rain at some point.

An even greater and more vital lesson we've learned through living in this unpredictable world is that we are walking in the Reign. At least, that is where we should be and where we should want to be.

As we journey through life, God in His infinite wisdom, knew we'd need guidance every step of the way. In His grace and mercy, He gave us the ability to speak to Him and hear from Him through prayer and through His Word. But He also went to the added effort of placing understanding within our reach by planting examples of His truth in the world around us. He made His invisible attributes to be seen and understood by the things He created.

And the beautiful thing about walking in the reign is that when we do, God will bless us with a downpouring of His wisdom. We'll be walking in the rain of truth while we walk in the reign of God.

What a loving God we serve as we walk wisely in His Reign. We pray that the words in this book will be an encouragement to you to always be on the lookout for the truth that rains when you are walking in the Reign.

Loving God

Walking in the Reign

1

The Breath of God

Yet to all who did receive him, to those who believed in his name,
he gave the right to become children of God (John 1:12 NIV).

A late afternoon sky stretched above us, a grayish-blue expanse mirrored by the sea as the two blended together on the far horizon. Caesarea today was calm, peaceful, humbling.

From our seats in the ancient Roman amphitheater, we watched ships sail by in the distance as a gentle ocean wind welcomed us in this place.

As the worship team sang "It's Your Breath," the gentle breeze blew over us, soft, warm, and filled with the smell of the ocean. The breath of God. Or at least it felt so to me. A physical touch from God as we worshiped in a place once filled with the darkness of a pagan culture. I doubt Herod the Great could have imagined that the magnificent port city he built here for his own glory would be the launching point from which Christianity would pour forth to the rest of the world. Though known as a brilliant architect, Herod lived his life as the epitome of evil. His rule was ruthless, vicious, and selfish.

My imagination was swept into the creative arms of my Heavenly Father as I felt the ocean breeze, listened to the words of the song, and pondered what life might have looked like from this very place some two thousand years ago.

It was in Caesarea that Pilate lived during the time of Jesus' earthly ministry. It was in Caesarea that Paul was imprisoned for two years before being taken to Rome.

But it was also in Caesarea that a centurion named Cornelius became known as the first non-Jew to become a Christian—the first gentile conversion to Christianity.

"At Caesarea there was a man named Cornelius, a centurion in what was known as the Italian Regiment. He and all his family were devout and God-fearing; he gave generously to those in need and prayed to God regularly" (Acts 10:1-2 NIV).

When we meet Cornelius in Acts, he is already a believer in the God of the Jews. How did this man—a Roman who fought on behalf of Rome with enough distinction to be promoted to centurion—first encounter God? The Bible doesn't tell us. We only get to experience his story from the time when the angel came to him in a dream, instructing him to send for Peter so that his faith might be fulfilled.

I couldn't help but wonder, though, if perhaps Cornelius might have stood in this very amphitheater and watched the sun set over the Mediterranean, knowing in his heart there was more. More than the ruthless vanity of Herod and the rulers who followed him. More than a constant striving for things that never seemed to fill the empty places.

Did he feel the breath of God blow over him as took his seat facing over the ocean?

Would he have looked around to see if anyone else had felt it? Or would he have looked in bewilderment at the crowd packed around him, recognizing what they could not see? Did he see dull eyes staring back at him from faces carved from lives without hope? Lost in their clamor for more because they could never be satisfied, their eyes blind to the truth written in the vibrant colors of the sunset sweeping across the horizon, their skin dull to the feel of the gentle breeze that whispered of a life beyond?

We don't know, but maybe he had a moment like this. Seated in a place built on the precepts of darkness, surrounded by the pagan influences of the day, God found him.

There is no place so dark, no person so lost or sinful, that God can't breathe hope and new life into him or her.

This is the glorious news of the gospel—and it's available for everyone.

Questions for Reflection:

In what ways have you felt God calling you to more: more of truth, more of faith, more of life?

How did He speak to you, and what was your response? Would you respond differently now?

2

Follow Me

Whoever serves me must follow me; and where I am, my servant also will be. My Father will honor the one who serves me (John 12:26 NIV).

"I'm not on the cross. Don't look for me there."

Asked to visualize the scene of the cross and then invite Jesus into our thoughts, I did as I was told. But Jesus didn't come. I just stared at the empty cross on a barren hill, wondering where He was. Everyone else participating in this creative exercise seemed to have no problem. What was wrong with me?

My now-troubled mind filled with thoughts: *Jesus, where are you? You have to show up so I can complete this exercise.*

And then I heard—only in my head but quite loud and clear— "I'm not on the cross. Why are you going there to find me?"

Was there a note of impatience in the voice? It didn't condemn, but the conviction was real.

God directed my attention from the empty cross to an outcropping of rock not far away. Seated atop this rock, waiting with infinite patience, was Jesus. Not Jesus in His flowing robe as we usually imagine Him, but Jesus in a flannel shirt and hiking boots. Jesus ready for action.

He wasn't resting, He was waiting. For me.

I wasn't sure I was still following through on the exercise correctly, but I no longer cared. I was having a sacred moment of revelation.

We've been reminded of the great sacrifice Jesus made by going to the cross to die on our behalf. We see the unfathomable love the Father has for us in this sacrifice, this atonement for our sins, making us holy and righteous as He is holy and righteous. How grateful we are, how in awe and amazement we stand. To be loved with such devotion and fierceness—a love like we have never experienced before and never will again this side of eternity. It is understandable that we want to linger in the place where it all happened.

We step from the cross to the empty tomb. Jesus rose from the dead to live, not just again, but forever with His Heavenly Father. Where the cross engulfs us in love, the empty tomb floods us with the glorious promise of eternal life with our Heavenly Father. What a perfect place to wait for eternity, a constant reminder that we have been made clean and death has no hold on us.

But therein lies the problem. Waiting....

We become focused on the beauty of the cross or the power of the empty tomb, and we forget what else Jesus said. In John 21:19 NIV, the risen Christ says to His disciples, *"Follow me!"*

He doesn't say, "Wait here until I get back."

If we only go as far as the cross and the empty tomb, we're only going to experience half the joy of what Christ has done for us.

What would it feel like if someone gave you an all-expenses paid trip to a tropical island, but you just stood there, reverently clutching the ticket and thanking them? How would they feel?

Perhaps you told them repeatedly how unworthy you were to receive such a gift. Then you poured everything you have into setting up a memorial to the moment they gave it to you. What if you never used the ticket to go on the journey you'd been invited to take?

After His resurrection, Jesus asked Peter, "Do you love me?" Three times, He asked Peter if he loved Him. Three times, Peter answered Him "Yes Lord." And three times, Jesus responded by telling Peter to feed and care for His sheep (see John 21).

I have a relationship with Jesus because someone first led me to the cross of Christ and then to the empty tomb. Someone was willing to feed His sheep. They didn't stay at the cross. They turned and saw Jesus leaving the tomb and followed Him over a rocky mountain path that, praise God, led them to me.

Am I going to keep staring at the vacant cross or empty tomb while Jesus sits nearby, checking His watch, adjusting the laces on His hiking boots, and wondering when I will finally realize it is finished, but I am not?

I've seen the Garden Tomb and the place of Calvary. I can verify the cross is gone and the tomb is still empty. The work Jesus asks of me isn't there, either. It is a beautiful, sacred place, both aesthetically and spiritually, but it is not the destination of my Christian walk. It is the ticket station into the journey and life Christ purchased for me.

"Follow me!"

Yes, Lord.

If the cross and the empty tomb don't ignite a passion in me for more, then I question if I really understand the significance of either.

Let us never forget that it is finished, but we are not.

Questions for Reflections:

> Who in your life has led you closer to Jesus? How did that person do this?

> What is one thing you could do today to feed one of God's sheep? How could you encourage someone to join you in this?

3

Tents in the Valley

(by Emily Dehm)

I will give thanks to the LORD because of his righteousness; I will sing the praises of the name of the LORD Most High (Psalm 7:17 NIV).

I have been thinking about valleys and mountaintops lately. Not just dreaming I was in the mountains I adore, although there have been a few times I had those mountains in mind.

My husband and I are in a bit of a valley right now. Or maybe nearing the part where it starts to get steep as we head toward the mountaintop.

And you wanna know a fun fact?

I have been Negative Nancy. I have dwelled on all the things that are "wrong." I have not shown this valley a single bit of appreciation. I have felt lost, confused, and forsaken. Instead of pressing on towards the mountaintop, I pitched a tent and took up permanent residence in the valley.

And while I'm sitting in my tattered tent, it occurs to me.

21

What if Jesus came back today? In this moment?

What if Jesus doesn't come back when I am praising Him on the top of the mountain but rather shaking my fist at Him in the valley?

I gave myself goosebumps with this thought.

I think we kind of just assume Jesus will come back when it is nice and convenient for us, and we are in good moods and life is rainbows and sunshine.

But what if He doesn't?

Are we praising Him in the lowest valleys? Are we abandoning the tent to run towards Him?

If you are anything like me, sometimes life just flat gets you down. It just does. Life is exhausting sometimes. And it has valleys and curves and difficulties.

But my God, the God I freely serve, brings me through it all, without a second thought. He didn't leave me in my valley tent.

Mountain high or valley low, He is still coming for us, to bring us to our eternal home. Sometimes, it's hard to praise when all you feel is defeat and confusion. But our weaknesses are avenues for God's strength to be shown.

The same way you must choose to delight in your weaknesses is the same way you must choose to praise in the valley that seems never-ending.

Delight in the Lord, remembering that if there were no valleys, there would be no mountaintops.

"Not that I have already obtained all this, or have already arrived at my goal, but I press on to take hold of that for which Christ Jesus took hold of me" (Philippians 3:12 NIV).

"Consider it pure joy, my brothers and sisters, whenever you face trials of many kinds, because you know that the testing of your faith produces perseverance" (James 1:2-3 NIV).

Questions for Reflection:

> What are the mountains that surround you when you feel trapped in a valley? Do you treat your "tent in the valley" as a permanent residence?

> What is one thing you could constantly praise even when you are in a valley?

4

Love Notes from God

You will seek me and find me when you seek me with all your heart
(Jeremiah 29:13 NIV).

God longs for us to pursue Him. He desires for us to see the evidence of His favor in the first light of dawn, in the dew on the grass and the web of the spider, in the taste of an apple, and the smell of honeysuckle on a warm evening breeze.

He delights to shower us in notes of His affection for us because He is teaching us to be pursued.

And He promises us that when we seek Him with our hearts, we will find Him.

Romance. We seek it in the books we read, the movies we watch, and the songs we listen to. But do we understand why the romance matters?

The desire to be romanced is the desire to be pursued. It is not a feminine weakness, insecurity, or fanciful wishing. It is a God-given gift that reveals His heart for us. Like the pursuit of a boyfriend or husband—and yet so much more. God longs for us to know He is pursuing us—relentlessly.

Jesus told three parables in which God was portrayed as a seeker (see Luke 15): the shepherd determinedly seeking a lost sheep, the woman turning the house upside down in search of a lost coin, and the father of the wayward son, forever watching the horizon for his son's return. In each story, the seeker was relentless. Something was so valuable to them it was worth searching for and going after until it was found.

And what joy came in the finding.

God seeks what is valuable to Him—us. But He doesn't demand our love. He woos us until it is freely given. God uses love notes to capture our attention and then our hearts when we let Him.

Oh, but He doesn't use a generic box of pre-made valentines. He created each of us as a one-of-a-kind original. He would never use a one-size-fits-all kind of note to express His love. As unique as we are in so many ways, so too God crafts His tailor-made love notes for each of us.

I have twins—a girl and a boy—and the only thing they have in common is they share the same birthday (and the same amazing mother—but that's a devotion for another time). He loves chocolate cake. She loves vanilla cake. I am not going to communicate my love to her by baking her a chocolate cake, nor would I let him know he was loved by baking him a vanilla cake. I speak to each of them in the individual ways I know mean the most to them. And yes, this does mean that we have two birthday cakes every November twenty-ninth—as if we weren't already stuffed full of Thanksgiving leftovers.

I know someone who says prime parking places are her love notes from God. I like to park a little farther out and walk. God isn't going to use a parking space for me. I wouldn't recognize it as a love note. It would be just another vacant spot of asphalt.

Isn't it wonderful that God loves us so much He knows exactly how to capture our attention and speak to our individual and unique hearts?

For me, a love note from God may be a gentle breeze, soft against my cheek, fluttering gently through my hair. It is the tender touch of love from the Creator to His creation. The One who knows me like no other because He formed me, knitting together my very being in my mother's womb.

How about sunsets, tulips, the taste of chocolate, or the sound of a child laughing? The smell of rain, light through a stained-glass window, a phone call from a friend, or just the right song on the radio at just the time we need to hear it?

God is romancing us, calling us to Him by delighting our souls with love notes that could only be from Him.

He waits with arms open wide, calling, "Come to me."

Questions for Reflection:

>What are some of the unique ways God romances you? What is the appropriate response to these moments?

>In what ways might God be romancing you that you've overlooked or taken for granted?

5

Troubled Waters and My Perspective

The disciples went and woke him, saying, "Master, Master, we're going to drown!" He got up and rebuked the wind and the raging waters; the storm subsided, and all was calm. "Where is your faith?" he asked his disciples (Luke 8:24-25 NIV).

Troubled waters. They got Jonah tossed overboard. They shipwrecked Paul more than once and sank Peter when he tried to walk on them.

But God used them every time.

A cruise is not the ideal vacation for someone who gets motion sickness. I know this now. Troubled waters at sea made me wonder why Jonah, Paul, and Peter were willing to ever get on a boat a second time. No, thanks. I'll just walk or stay home.

I remember quite clearly the troubled waters I experienced the one time when I went on a cruise. I didn't just see them from the relative safety of the lido deck. I was forced to walk the gangplank across them. Seriously.

We took a shore excursion and had to transfer from our cruise ship to another boat at sea amidst winds that were rocking these boats all over the place. I mean, this made *The Perfect Storm* look like a jaunt in a nice tropical breeze (my completely objective assessment of the situation). This board—was it any wider than a two-by-four? —with some flimsy, rope rails to hold on to was our passageway between two giant hunks of metal thrashing about as water splashed everywhere. And do you know what the attendant helping us across said to me?

"Watch your head." This was their biggest concern, really? I was about to become shark food, but apparently sharks don't like lumpy heads. Trust me, my head was the least of my worries. I looked down at certain death below me. Troubled waters, indeed. I would have told them this if I hadn't been afraid to open my mouth (recall the aforementioned sea sickness).

But by telling me to watch my head, the attendant drew my attention from the water below me to something above me. I looked up. He shifted my focus and gave me a new perspective.

A few years ago, I did the sensible thing and enjoyed a body of water from the shore of a lake. It was a breezy, autumn day and the winds were definitely troubling the waters. The choppy waves gave the lake's surface a dark, agitated, rough look. Even a bit gloomy and depressing. Then I turned my head in the other direction.

And that's when I saw thousands of bright, white sparkles as the sun glinted off these same waves. Perspective.

By changing mine, I allowed the sun's rays to shine on these troubled waters, and now I saw something altogether different. This was no gloomy, depressing, dark water. It was alive and glittering as if thousands of diamonds danced across its surface.

Perspective. When I allow the Son's light to shine on the troubled waters of my life—a difficult relationship, physical limitation, workplace environment—I allow God to show me something beautiful He is working out in the bigger picture.

My troubles become the canvas where God paints His glory. I need only to let the Son's light shine upon my life—in trouble and tranquility—for the glittering of thousands of diamonds to dance across its surface.

Questions for Reflection:

> How might certain areas or problems in your life look different from a changed perspective?

> How might God use your problems as a canvas for His glory?

6

Waterfalls and a Holy Hush

Whether you turn to the right or to the left, your ears will hear a voice behind you, saying, "This is the way; walk in it"
(Isaiah 30:21 NIV).

Waterfalls. A combination of gravity and water that calls to the soul and draws me like a magnet, although I don't understand why. Whether it's a small mountain stream trickling down a slope in the forest, or a massive river pouring from the top of a cliff I can barely see, there's something captivating in a waterfall. Its beauty demands my awe, but God can also teach me something from a waterfall.

Not all falling water inspires the same sense of wonder. The sound of water falling from the faucet over a pile of dirty dishes in my sink does not at all produce the same excitement, much less awe. And I've never witnessed anyone in my family being drawn to the kitchen because they heard water falling into the sink. We may pull out our map and hiking poles in search of a waterfall, but no one has ever leapt from the table after a meal in search of the kitchen faucet.

However, if there's a waterfall listed within a fifty-mile radius of wherever we are, we're on our way. Finding a waterfall is better than a pot full of gold at the end of a rainbow.

Sometimes, we set out knowing there is a waterfall to be found, but other times we come across one unexpectedly. Whichever way it happens, it is always true that we are aware of the waterfall's existence before we stand in its presence. A whisper of sound, at first barely audible, swells to a roar as we come closer.

Our walk with God is like finding the waterfall. We may hear Him first in a faint whisper, drawing our attention to His presence in our lives. We may have to strain to hear it, focusing our attention, wondering if that is what we really hear. We train our senses in the direction we think we need to go, tuning out every other sound.

We take a step, trying to determine which way to proceed. A misstep, and the whisper grows quieter. We readjust our path, sometimes returning to the place we started, until the sound is heard again. We take one step after another, following the gentle murmur as it becomes louder and louder. The closer we get, the clearer His voice becomes. Finally, we stand in His presence, so close the mighty roar of His voice is the only thing we hear.

It is then and there we experience the holy hush of God's voice speaking into our hearts. I believe it is the kind of conversation He longs to have with us. One where no other distractions can be heard. His voice alone has our undivided attention.

Maybe I do understand after all why my heart responds to waterfalls the way it does.

At the base of the waterfall, I stand on sacred ground.

Questions for Reflection:

What does the presence of the Lord sound like to you? Where do you hear Him speaking to you most often? How does it make you feel?

What distractions get in the way and divert your attention? How can they be silenced?

7

Warming My Soul

Arise, shine; For your light has come! And the glory of the Lord is risen upon you (Isaiah 60:1 NKJV).

Winter in Texas is as predictable as a monkey on Mountain Dew. Thirty degrees one day, eighty the next. Or worse, eighty in the morning and thirty by lunch. People in Texas do not plan out the weeks' worth of outfits on Sunday night.

As I write this, we have experienced a string of days where the temperatures never got out of the upper twenties, with drizzle and freezing rain. Miserably cold. In Texas, these are the conditions that inspire panic, food hoarding, the updating of wills, and gas shortages.

But as quickly as it came, the cold left, and the sun shone through. After having spent several days writing in the climate-controlled comfort of my office, I headed out to catch what warmth from the sunlight I could. As soon as I stepped into the light, the warmth of the winter sun wrapped around me like the embrace of a lover.

I turned to face the sun. I closed my eyes and let the rays soak into my soul. The heat of the summer sun hits a person all at once like a furnace blast. But the winter sun reaches through the chilly air, settling against one's skin like golden, warm honey soaking into a slice of freshly baked bread.

Tension in my body I wasn't aware of released. My arms fell open, hanging loose and ready to receive. I felt the radiance of God's love washing over me.

Then a commotion behind me—the dog and cat were having a disagreement about who should be closest to me, I think—captured my attention. Distracted, I turned to look, my back now to the sun. The soul satisfying warmth disappeared in an instant, much faster than it came. I wrapped my arms around my middle, holding myself tightly, trying to protect myself from the chill that instantly took its place.

In that moment, I realized just how easily I do the same with God.

I turn my face to Him and feel His love radiating through me. I relax my anxious worrying. I stand open to receive whatever He has for me. I rest in His abundant love.

Then something distracts me, and I turn my attention away from Him. Maybe it's an unexpected event—a diagnosis, job change, or prodigal child. Or it could be a series of small things turning me slowly by degrees. An overcommitted schedule. A wounded heart I refuse to address. A television show I won't stop watching or friends who pull me toward things that aren't God's best for me. Soon my arms no longer hang open to receive from God. I hug them tightly against me for protection, guarding my fragile soul. My body becomes tense, uncomfortable, and cold.

Now, I have a choice. I can grow accustomed to the cold, learning to live with the ache until I accept it as normal. I can let the unexpected event hold my attention captive. I can continue filling my schedule with things that rob me of my time with God. I can nurse a grudge by refusing to forgive or cling to relationships that pull me away from God. And I'm sure that for each of these things I can develop a perfectly wonderful excuse or argument to justify my choice.

Or I can choose to turn back to the Son.

In the book of Revelation, Jesus warns the church at Ephesus with these words:

"Yet I hold this against you: You have forsaken the love you had at first. Consider how far you have fallen! Repent and do the things you did at first" (Revelation 2:4-5 NIV).

These words as easily apply to us when we allow things— sometimes even good things—to take our attention from God. But the good news is that it doesn't have to be a permanent condition.

Jesus is always there, always ready to welcome us back into His fellowship when we repent.

Oh, the unmistakable beauty found in the everyday rising of the sun. Is it possible that God has established this as an example for us? The Son is always there. We have only to turn to Him and be warmed.

Turn your face to Him today and embrace the warmth of His love.

Questions for Reflection:

What things are turning your attention away from God?

If you feel the chill of a separation from God's love right now, how might you step back into the warmth of His love?

8

Is Jesus Your Lord or Your Lure?

(by Emily Dehm)

All a person's ways seem pure to them, but motives are weighed by the LORD (Proverbs 16:2 NIV).

I want to share something with you, and it may very nearly knock your socks off, but please brace yourselves because this is of high importance.

Self-promotion is a sin.

pause to process this information

Self-promotion is contradicting God. We are to promote Him, build His kingdom, not our own. Yes, that means exactly what you think it means.

We are not the point.

God did not create us to do great and mighty works for ourselves, He created us to do great and mighty works for HIM.

People often use their Christianity to promote their business, their life adventures, to "make it okay." He isn't here to promote our businesses. Jesus isn't here to cover for us. He isn't our alibi so we can do whatever we want and tack His name on it and make it less sinful.

I cannot build my own little kingdom and cover it up by proclaiming that I am promoting Jesus. It simply doesn't work that way. We live in a fallen, broken world that tells us to promote ourselves above all. The enemy tells us that we can build our kingdom first, and once that is solid, maybe we can move on to building God's. Or even worse, he tells us that by building ours, we are building God's.

By this time, of course, we are so deep into self-promotion that it is all we know. We speak it. We post it. We live it.

And God's kingdom continues to be built without a single brick touched by us.

Do you know that a person with purpose doesn't have to chase people, opportunities, or make people believe that he or she has it all together? A person with purpose lets God shine His light so brightly through them that opportunities and people simply follow.

Picture the way you see bugs attracted to light. Flowers that grow toward sunlight.

When God's light is in us, there is no need to self-promote. There is no need to build our own kingdom.

When we are content in Jesus Christ, our soul is satisfied. We want nothing more than to build His glorious kingdom with every second of our lives. The life He has blessed us with.

Make a choice.

Promote ourselves or promote God?

Whose kingdom am I choosing to build?

Every day of our lives, we lay bricks toward a kingdom. It is up to us to figure out which kingdom it is.

Questions for Reflection:

Who do you find it easier to promote—yourself or God?

Who or what do your actions promote? Are you satisfied with the results?

9

Seeing or Experiencing

...and all who touched it were healed (Matthew 14:36 NIV).

There's a significant difference between seeing something and experiencing something.

We can see a mountain, or we can climb a mountain. Only by setting out on the trail will we find the beauty hidden deep in the forest or know the strength and determination it takes to ascend.

We can see the ocean, or we can stand in the ocean. Only by standing in the water will we feel the cool refreshment it offers or know the power of the rushing waves.

The difference between seeing and experiencing is the difference between being alive and living—the difference between wishing for joy and actually reaching for joy.

In the passage above from Matthew 14, people came from all around, bringing their sick to Jesus for healing. They begged Him to just let the sick touch His cloak.

Scripture says, *"...all who touched it were healed."* Not all who came or saw or heard. Only those who reached out in faith and touched Jesus received healing.

If reaching out and touching His cloak was all that was needed, why weren't they all healed? What held some back from this one simple, life-changing act of faith? Was it possible they had a faith so small a shadow of doubt kept it from action?

Faith is an action.

And Jesus says faith as small as a mustard seed is all it takes (see Matthew 17:20).

There is seeing but not experiencing in our churches and our world today. We pray the prayer of salvation, read our Bible, and partake in communion. We go to church, hear the sermon, and sing along with the worship team or choir. And when we don't experience the healing we long for or a joy that surpasses understanding, we wonder what's wrong with the church or Christianity in general. Why aren't we healed from our anxieties, our fears, our depression?

We see Jesus, but do we reach out to touch Him?

A few years ago, I went through a season of being in a dry place. I couldn't seem to find my way out. It was during this time God kept leading me to the story of the woman with the bleeding disorder. She risked her life to go out in public and reach for Jesus.

To understand the level of desperation she felt, we must understand that in those days her condition made her unclean, and that was just about as despised a condition as anyone could have in those days. Anyone she came in contact with would likewise become unclean, a status that came with a lot of unpleasant restrictions and burdensome actions needed to restore their status as clean. Her presence in a crowd was a highly punishable offense.

But still she came.

Still she reached out.

Still she took hold in the faith that risking it all to touch Jesus was worth the price she might pay. She knew it wasn't enough to hear about Jesus or see Jesus. She wanted to touch Him, feel His presence, to participate in the reality of His power.

"For she said to herself, 'If only I may touch His garment, I shall be made well'" (Matthew 9:21 NKJV).

Her healing came through her faith as she reached out to touch Jesus, and through that one small touch, His healing flowed into her brokenness.

This message soaked into me with the gentle ease of a sledgehammer. What I was doing was watching Jesus from afar. Like a spectator in the bleachers, I knew the players and how to run the plays. I cheered for "my team" and declared my allegiance with a logo on my T-shirt, but I certainly wasn't in the game. I wasn't partaking in the life of Christ. I was watching.

Watching wouldn't heal what was missing in my life. I had to reach out and touch Jesus. And to touch Him, I had to go where He was. I had to participate in the reality of His power.

We can read God's Word and memorize it like the words are a magic incantation that will heal us or fill us with peace and joy. But if the Scriptures aren't a doorway to us through which we enter a personal and intimate conversation with Jesus—so close we can touch Him—then they are nothing more than words on paper.

Like the woman with the bleeding disorder, what will it take to make us desperate enough to reach out to Jesus for the healing we long for?

Questions for Reflection:

> Are there doubts keeping you from acting in faith? How might your life be changed if you exercised faith despite your doubts?

> Are you walking close enough to Jesus to touch Him? What would it look like to experience His healing power in your life right now? What are you willing to risk?

10

Who Told You to Turn Off the Navigation?

I will instruct you and teach you in the way you should go; I will counsel you with my loving eye on you (Psalm 32:8 NIV).

I have never understood why the very first thing my vehicle's navigation system feels compelled to tell me is, "Follow the road." Is it worried I might drive through the neighbor's front yard instead? I think perhaps my GPS has control issues. And if you know me, you know how I feel about control issues.

Of course, there is a time to admit our weaknesses and seek dependable guidance.

Recently, I found myself driving home from a writing conference in Oklahoma City on Labor Day. Since the trip would take me through the holiday weekend traffic of Fort Worth, I decided to program my navigation to take me home along a less congested route through the country. A friend recommended an app for my phone that would not only direct me but warn me of things like cars parked on the side of the road or dangerous debris in my lane. This app told me everything—and it got annoying.

I reached the last major turn I was unfamiliar with and knew it was a straight shot down to the next town about thirty miles away. From there, I easily knew my way home. Finally, I felt confident in turning off the pesky voice that kept interrupting my music. What could possibly go wrong?

Well, let's review a few things that could possibly go wrong. For starters, I have terrible night vision and it was almost dark. And while I was currently on the correct road, I failed to notice that there were two highways joined there. The one I needed to continue taking would split off in a few miles. And we can't leave out the fact that I am somewhat lacking in my sense of direction.

To make a long story short, I made a long trip even longer. I missed my turn and ended up driving in the exact opposite direction I needed to go. I was headed right toward the place I had gone out of my way to avoid.

I now had plenty of driving time to consider the error of my ways. I thought about all the times I do this with God. He is my perfect guide. He alone knows the path I'm meant to take and what lies ahead.

But sometimes, I get a few miles of smooth, easy travel and allow overconfidence to influence my decisions. Maybe it's a situation I've faced many times before. I think I've got it handled—no need to pray about it this time.

How about when I am reading a devotion or Bible study and I skim over, or even skip, reading the Scripture passage because it's one I know already, and well…, I'm in a hurry? The conviction of that one stung quite a bit.

In my overconfidence, I stop listening to the only voice that sees the path before me and can guide me safely home.

Suddenly, I've missed a turn and find myself careening into trouble that could have been avoided.

Thankfully when this happens, if I allow Him to, God will always guide me back to the right path. First, I repent—I stop going in the direction I'm headed. Then I turn the GPS—God Positioning System—back on through prayer and Bible reading.

God's Word isn't meant to bore us with trivial observations or repetition. If He says it, then it is significant.

There is no way we can go, no path we can know so well, that God's direction isn't still needed. He alone knows what lies ahead.

Questions for Reflection:

> What areas of your life do you try to navigate on your own? What do you lack that makes this a bad idea?
>
> How do you stay tuned in to God's guidance in your life?

Walking in the Reign

Loving Others

Walking in the Reign

11

I Walked Where Jesus Walked

Then he said to him, "Follow me!" (John 21:19 NIV).

Two weeks in Israel exploring the people and places of biblical history, soaking in a bit of Jewish culture, setting my feet in the very places Jesus walked during the days of His ministry on earth. Not just the places He could've been or might've been, but places where Scripture tells us He was.

The synagogue in ancient Capernaum. The Pools of Bethesda. The Southern Steps leading up to the Temple Mount. Scripture tells us specifically Jesus was here. To walk in these places is both humbling and indescribably beautiful.

I came here to learn more about His ministry and teachings. I came to gain better understanding of Scripture by experiencing these places. I came hoping to feel closer to Jesus by physically touching the same places He touched.

And in each of these desires, Jesus found me and blessed me beyond anything I could have asked.

Yes, I walked where Jesus walked, and He walked with me.

But have I really walked where Jesus walked?

This is the question God kept whispering in my ear.

Have I truly walked where Jesus walked?

"But Jesus said to them, 'A prophet is not without honor except in his own town and in his own home'" (Matthew 13:57 NIV).

Have I stood before the doubters and the skeptics and poured my heart out in the often-vain hope they would hear, understand, and accept salvation? Or have I let fear of rejection or judgment keep me from sharing the gospel with my family, friends, neighbors, and coworkers who need to hear the good news?

"While Jesus was having dinner at Matthew's house, many tax collectors and sinners came and ate with him and his disciples" (Matthew 9:10 NIV).

Have I welcomed the company of the unpopular, the unwanted, the despised and forgotten? Have I been willing to go to them, or am I content to merely go to the edge of their world and try to wave them over into mine? To stand at the edge of their neighborhood and hope they'll come out?

"Then Jesus put out His hand and touched him, saying, 'I am willing; be cleansed.' Immediately his leprosy was cleansed'" (Matthew 8:3NKJV).

Have I gone to the sick and unclean with a willing heart and sought to comfort them or help them at the expense of my comfort or security?

"Then Jesus said, 'Father forgive them for they do not know what they do'" (Luke 23:34 NKJV).

Have I interceded in prayer for my enemies?

"And when He had spoken this, He said to him, 'Follow Me'" (John 21:19 NKJV).

Have I forgiven those who have betrayed me?

"Now as He drew near, He saw the city and wept over it, saying, 'If you had known, even you, especially in this your day, the things that make for your peace! But now they are hidden from your eyes'" (Luke 19:41-42 NKJV).

Have I wept over Jerusalem as Jesus did?

It is a sacred experience to visit the Holy Land, but it is not the ultimate destination. When Jesus said, *"Follow me,"* this is not the journey He spoke of.

Follow me…

…to walk among the lost and forgotten,

…to walk among the sick and unclean,

…to walk among the poor and hopeless,

…to walk among the hateful and hostile,

…to walk among the broken and unseen.

These are the places Jesus walked and calls us to walk today.

Our tour guide told us we weren't just walking through Israel. Israel was walking through us. But if I really soak in the deeper meaning of these words, I understand it also means I wasn't just walking where Jesus walked. Jesus was walking through me. It's the place He has always headed, isn't it?

Now, I'm back home, and I can no longer step in Jesus' physical footsteps, but I can let Him continue to walk through me, taking me to the places He calls me to go.

Questions for Reflection:

What does it mean to walk where Jesus walked?

What opportunities can you find to walk where Jesus walked? Do you hesitate? If so, why and how might you change your perspective on the situation?

12

The Temple Steps

But whenever anyone turns to the Lord, the veil is taken away. Now the Lord is the Spirit, and where the Spirit of the Lord is, there is freedom. And we all, who with unveiled faces contemplate the Lord's glory, are being transformed into his image with ever-increasing glory, which comes from the Lord, who is the Spirit (2 Corinthians 3:16-18 NIV).

When we accept Jesus as our Lord and Savior, we are sanctified, meaning set apart for the glory of God. But it also means we enter a continual process of sanctification—moving from one degree of glory to another.

If being transformed into the image of Christ is our goal, then we must get there one step at a time.

After I accepted Jesus as my Lord and Savior, my life became a continual process of sanctification process. To realize the fullness of that sanctification, I must nurture a thirst for more, continually seeking the next level of understanding, the next level of glory. There is always another step.

The Southern Steps of the Temple Mount in Jerusalem are known as the Teaching Steps. Rabbis could be found teaching and instructing here. Jesus surely would have taught here. Scholars also believe this is the place where the church was born in Acts 2 on the day of Pentecost.

As I stood on these steps looking over the ancient City of David and the steep climb from there to the Temple Mount, I could see the bottom step was just as necessary and important as the one at the top. If we didn't take the first step, we'd never take the last.

From one degree of glory to the next. Steps. And we need every step in its place in order to reach the destination.

One of the ways I learn, explore, and go deeper in my own faith is through writing. And if I can share anything with you that encourages, informs, inspires, or enlightens you in a way that stirs your desire for more of God, then I have honored my gift. If what you read here causes you to take another step, then I am more than happy for you to take it even if it means you are moving beyond what I can offer.

Take the next step.

I never want to lose sight of the fact that I am only a rung on someone else's ladder—a step on their climb to the temple mount. God has created me to fit in a specific place on this ladder. There is no shame in being useful to another right where I am in the moment.

If you've ever tried to climb a ladder with any of the rungs missing, you understand that not only is it challenging and risky, but it also slows you down and sometimes stops you completely.

We are all equipped to be a rung on someone else's ladder. We may fulfill different levels with different people, but the reality is that if we aren't in place, if we aren't willing to be the next step, then there's a rung missing in someone else's ladder.

Until we take the final step into eternity, there is always another step to take. No one this side of eternity has attained the final glory because it is meant to be ours in heaven.

What joy it is to be a step, lifting another in his or her climb to Glory.

And what a blessing to know that the bottom step is no less important than the one at the top.

Questions for Reflection:

> Do you need help taking the next step in your walk with God? Where might you go or what action could you take to find that help?

> What are the ways you could help someone else from right where you are by being a rung on their ladder?

13

Welcoming Intrusion

(by Emily Dehm)

There is a time for everything, and a season for every activity under the heavens (Ecclesiastes 3:1 NIV).

I do not like having my agenda derailed. I do not like having my plans interrupted, changed, or messed with in any way, shape, or form. I wake in the morning with a checklist, and I want to draw a bright, blue mark next to each task by the end of the day. I have set goals, plans, and a specific way they should all be handled.

I do not like intrusion.

And that is a problem.

You see, at the end of the day, I'm either promoting my agenda or promoting God's.

Now, I know that seems super dramatic, and even a bit of a stretch, but bear with me a minute.

Jesus constantly welcomed intrusion in his life. He washed feet, He healed, He listened, and He loved. He was not concerned about His agenda, His travels, or who came to intrude upon His day.

When the unclean, bleeding woman came to Him in desperation, He stopped what He was doing and healed her.

Jesus didn't put his hand up in annoyance, saying, "Excuse me, miss, but you are interrupting my day's schedule, and I don't have time for this right now. Call me later, and I can pencil you in for next week."

Jesus knew He was on this earth for one purpose…to do the will of God. He was entirely unbothered by this intrusion. Jesus did not have a mile-long checklist. He had only two tasks: to love and to serve.

What a beautiful reminder this is for us, especially on the days that are filled with all kinds of intrusion and disruption. (Like when you are prepping for a colonoscopy and simultaneously come down with a sinus infection. ALL kinds of disruption. I still cannot drink Gatorade or eat Jell-O.)

I know how hard it is to relinquish control of our plans and agendas. In fact, it is a legitimate struggle every single morning. I desire to lay out my perfect plan for the day. Everyone follows the script, it will be a great day. I cling to what I personally think is the best option, the best course of action.

I remember playing dodgeball in P.E. and thinking what absolute chaos it was. Brightly colored, incredibly painful dodgeballs whizzed through the air at anything that moved. People were screaming, running, throwing. I remember how relieved I was when I got hit because after the stinging stopped, I could just chill on the mesh, plastic floor until the end of class. I was no longer captive to that chaos.

I think that when we desperately hang onto our own agendas and resist intrusion, we feel like dodgeballs are flying around us like heat-seeking missiles, waiting to make contact—and it's going to sting. But then we realize that it is truly exhausting, and we remove ourselves from the chaos we created, sit down on the ground, and let God do what God does best—be God.

God did not place us here to promote our schedules, agendas, and plans. He never once promised us an intrusion-free life. I'm so thankful that God allows us to intrude upon Him, day in and day out. He doesn't require three to five business days' notice. He doesn't give us one of those little things that buzzes when our table is ready. He doesn't tell us to come back on Monday.

We delight His heart when we intrude upon Him, casting our burdens and cares at His feet.

Welcome the intrusions, friends. Welcome the delays, the interruptions, and the divine interventions.

Jesus, the Son of God, the one person who could have brushed off each intrusion with complete immunity, welcomed it all.

Questions for Reflection:

Have you viewed your time as your own? How has this influenced the way you react to disruptions and intrusions? Do you view them as aggravations or opportunities?

How might your response to interruptions look differently if you saw your time as belonging to God?

14

The Power of Our Words

Likewise, the tongue is a small part of the body, but it makes great boasts. Consider what a great forest is set on fire by a small spark (James 3:5 NIV).

As I write this, one of my favorite places to be—the mountains of northern New Mexico—is on fire. We go there every year—to explore, to hike, to discover, to just *be*. It always brings us to an adventure.

I'm not sure why I love this area of the country so much. All I know is that I get a sense of peace there I don't get anywhere else. I hear God speak to me there, and my soul comes away refreshed.

On one of our annual summer trips, God had me pondering the beauty of the forest. I never grow tired of looking at it, exploring it, experiencing it.

A Christmas tree farm is full of trees too. But it's not the same. It is filled with the kinds of trees that inhabit the mountain forest. And in its own way, it has a sweet, nostalgic sort of beauty. But it is not the same.

The mountain forest is diverse, containing a variety of species and an infinite number of sizes and shapes within those species. It is the coming together, this diversity, that speaks to my soul, holds my attention, overwhelms me with its magnificence, fills my heart with love for the Creator.

Why then does the diversity of mankind not prompt a similar emotion?

As a society we spend countless hours and dollars striving for uniformity. A certain size, a certain shape, a certain hair color or style of dress. And when we lack the confidence that we have, or even can, achieve it, we lash out with words to destroy that which is different.

Scripture tells us that *"a great forest is set on fire by a small spark. The tongue also is a fire, a world of evil among the parts of the body"* (James 3:5-6 NIV). With it we can bring destruction and desolation, tearing apart the inherent beauty instilled in humanity by the same One who created the forest to be breathtakingly beautiful in its diversity.

Is it possible that our uniqueness, our individuality, is meant to be viewed as part of the whole of mankind? That we each have a special and distinct beauty that needs to be brought to and viewed in light of the spectacular whole?

A tapestry sewn with only one color of thread would be a pretty dull tapestry. A cake baked with ingredients that were all identical would just be...well...a bowl of baked flour.

The next time I visit the mountains in New Mexico, I will drive by places where the charred skeletons of the forest stand as a reminder of how little it takes to destroy something beautiful. One small spark. A malicious word. A careless comment. Perhaps Mordecai said it best when he told Esther she should not think that she alone would escape the coming destruction (see Esther 4:13).

I want to remember that I stand in the same forest I may be setting on fire with my words. The humanity I destroy may be my own.

This is a fire that doesn't need an investigation to determine its cause. We have an enemy who loves the smell of smoke and the feel of ashes. We must refuse to be used as his matchstick.

May our words fall like life-giving rain instead.

Questions for Reflection:

What words have been spoken over you that have wounded your soul?

What words would bring healing to your soul? What words could bring healing to someone else's soul?

15

Giving Directions

...yet in the church I would rather speak five words with my understanding, that I may teach others also, than ten thousand words in a tongue (1 Corinthians 14:19 NKJV).

The Mamertine prison—not a prison like we imagine. This prison was a dark, damp, rock-encased hole in the ground, a repurposed cistern or collecting place for water. Confinement in this would have been a hell on earth, if you survived the twenty-five-foot drop from the hole in the ceiling. This is the place where Peter, and possibly Paul, were held before being executed by Nero.

And it was on our list of things we wanted to see while in Rome. It is not, however, a much-mentioned or well-advertised sightseeing attraction. Go figure.

Locating it was more of a challenge than we anticipated. We studied the map forward and backward—and possibly upside down. We studied translations trying to understand the street names. If you've never been to Rome and want to understand their street system, dump a bowl of spaghetti noodles on the table, pick one, and try to follow it all the way to the end. The good news is there was a gelato store on every corner. If nothing else, we wouldn't go hungry. And we far exceeded our Fitbit step count goal for the day.

Finally, we had no choice. We could only eat so much gelato in a day while we looked. Rome just wasn't the easiest place to decipher. I mean, the place is a ruin.

The map appeared to be indicating the prison was somewhere close to the Forum, a section of ruins that is fenced off and requires a paid admission. We thought maybe we would find it there, and if not, maybe they could tell us how to find it.

Language isn't a complete barrier there thanks to the Romans doing a better job of learning a second language than we seem to do with our first here in the States. I approached the young woman in the ticket booth and explained to her—I thought—that we were having trouble finding the Mamertine prison. From there the conversation went like this:

Her: You want to see the Mamertine prison?

Me: Yes, that is correct.

Her: Then you should go there.

Me: * Blink * Blink *

In her defense, I don't believe she was trying to be flippant. And I really couldn't argue with her logic. What she said was the spot-on truth. Not one tiny bit helpful, but true, nonetheless.

Want to know how we finally found the prison? After skirting construction fences and wandering down unmarked sidewalks that came to a dead end, we gave up. And when, in defeat, we turned around to make the long walk back to the hotel, there in front of us was a sign in big, bold letters for the Mamertine prison. It was one of the most terrible places I'm glad I got to visit.

It did make me think about giving directions to others.

When someone comes to me for help, am I listening to them or just hearing them? Understanding requires more than just listening with my ears.

Do I understand what the real question or issue is before I offer an answer? Do I need to ask questions for clarity?

Am I able to respond in a way they'll understand? We may all attend the same church, but that doesn't mean we all use our words the same. There will be age, educational, geographical, and cultural factors that can get in the way of understanding.

When I am in a position to minister to someone, I can be guilty of telling them the truth but not helping them with an answer. Like the young lady at the ticket booth, I can give an answer that is absolutely true and not one bit helpful.

The apostle Paul says in First Corinthians, *"I thank my God I speak with tongues more than you all; yet in the church I would rather speak five words with my understanding, that I may teach others also, than ten thousand words in a tongue"* (1 Corinthians 14:18-19 NKJV).

How powerful and effective would our communications—and indeed, our relationships—be if speaking five words with our understanding was our goal each time we opened our mouths to give directions or help someone?

Questions for Reflection:

> Do you listen with a desire to understand? Or do you catch yourself just waiting for your chance to respond?
>
> How can we make sure our answers are helpful?

16

In the Flow

"A new command I give you: Love one another. As I have loved you, so you must love one another" (John 13:34 NIV).

Being in the flow. Webster's dictionary tells us to flow means to circulate, to move with a continual change of place among the constituent particles.

Jesus was in the flow.

In John 13:34 NIV, He says, *"A new command I give you: Love one another. As I have loved you, so you must love one another."*

"…so you must love one another."

Jesus loves us, and so we must love others. Seems simple enough. Unfortunately, we are often tempted to be more like a dam in the river, keeping this precious gift for ourselves and stingily doling out tiny bits on others.

Jesus' next statement is that, "By this all people will know that you are my disciples, if you have love for one another" (John 13:35 NKJV).

By this—loving others—people will know we are His disciples.

Not by what we accumulate, but by what we give.

The Dead Sea is the epitome of what happens when we hoard something for ourselves. It is fed by the Jordan River bringing water down from the Sea of Galilee. The Sea of Galilee is a freshwater lake around which much of the New Testament takes place. This lake abounds in life. During the times of Jesus' ministry, it provided the livelihood of multitudes of fishermen.

This same water flows out of the lake and down the Jordan until it reaches the Dead Sea, but with no outlet, the Dead Sea holds on to all it is given. The water becomes too toxic for life. Nothing lives there. The Dead Sea doesn't give.

It is not enough to accept God's love. We must have an outlet for it. To really be in the flow, we need to be a conduit. A channel through which God's love is conveyed.

The pouring out of this love makes it possible for us to give other things as well.

Forgiveness. Encouragement. Hope. Creativity.

Do you want to receive forgiveness? Then forgive.

Do you want encouragement? Then encourage.

Do you want to be known as a disciple? Nothing defines you as one more than the love you give.

The Jordan River is a conduit that allows the water in the Sea of Galilee to flow down into the Dead Sea. And what shapes the river? The power of the water flowing through gives it its shape. And the power of God's love flowing to us was shaped as a baby in a manger and the Messiah on a cross.

I want to look like the love of God and the life of Christ—a river of love flowing without ceasing.

Questions for Reflections:

In what ways are you serving as a conduit for God's love?

Are there areas in your life where you feel like the Dead Sea? What might you be hoarding for fear of losing?

17

Choosing Grace

(by Emily Dehm)

For the joy set before him he endured the cross, scorning its shame, and sat down at the right hand of the throne of God. Consider him who endured such opposition from sinners, so that you will not grow weary and lose heart (Hebrews 12:2-3 NIV).

You know that sinking feeling you get in your heart when you have been overlooked, left out, ignored?

You try so desperately not to be left out, but that seems to be the constant narrative of your life.

It can create tiny cracks in our hearts, and before we know it, we are broken.

How we respond in these situations is incredibly important. I write this with the utmost conviction because I have often experienced first-hand the pain and hurt of being brushed to the side, ignored, or left out.

It happens.

The world isn't perfect. We all feel the aftermath.

But how I respond is a choice I get to make.

My initial reaction is to feel anger and offense. I want to take each pointed word as a personal attack on my heart, soul, and life.

I want to lash out at the offender, make him or her accountable for the words and actions that make me feel this way. I want to point it out and throw it right back.

However, God commands us to respond with grace.

He isn't asking us to be doormats for aggressive people but to simply not take it so personally. To not let it define our lives. When someone says something that you could easily take offense to, ask yourself if it's worth being miserable over.

Is it worth having unrest in your soul?

Better yet, is it even true in light of all God says is true about us?

Choosing to forgive and extend grace to someone for their hurtful actions or deliberate neglect is often the toughest choice we can make.

But to respond with grace is to respond with God.

Jesus was betrayed, berated, and brutally beaten before being left to die. Yet in His dying breaths, He uttered, *"Forgive them, for they know not what they do" (Luke 23:34 NKJV)*.

If Jesus, as He hung nailed to the cross, was able not to take the persecution of the world to His soul, then can't we do the same? He forgave these people because He was confident in His eternity—and in His identity.

It isn't about changing the person's behavior. In fact, it typically doesn't. But it always changes yours. It humbles our hearts.

Instead of seeking the opportunity to become angry or offended, seek the opportunity to show love and grace to those who persecute you. Forgiving those who are not sorry, or possibly are even unaware of the effect of their actions, is one of the purest forms of our Godly obedience, proof we know our true identity.

Choose grace, y'all. It changes your heart in the deepest way and draws you so much nearer to the heart of God.

Questions for Reflection:

> What past hurts still reside in your heart? Who haven't you been able to forgive and why? How are these things affecting your life spiritually?

> How might you experience freedom in forgiving someone who has hurt you?

18

All About God

*Let nothing be done through selfish ambition or conceit, but in
lowliness of mind let each esteem others better than himself
(Philippians 2:3 NKJV).*

Visiting the top of Jungfrau was high on our list of things to do while
in Switzerland. Unfortunately, we arrived at the train station only to
find that a tunnel had collapsed, and nobody was going to the top of
Jungfrau for an undetermined amount of time.

This was somewhat disappointing to me because I rehearsed "The
hills are alive with the sound of music," for days and figured the top
of Jungfrau was going to be the ideal spot to unveil my musical
masterpiece.

But I also knew that for my husband, it was going to be a big
disappointment. He had been talking about this experience for
weeks, and today was our only opportunity on this trip to make it
happen. That's not the stuff my husband is made of, though. He
knew Jungfrau in and of itself was not what he longed for most. It
was only another sacred moment with God he wanted, and if God

wanted to show him something other than the top of Jungfrau, he was good with that too. God closed the tunnel so He could open a door.

We took the train to the last stop before the collapsed tunnel. Then we spent a couple of hours hiking on Eiger. Yes, I can truthfully say I've hiked on the legendary mountain of Eiger. Okay, just the safe parts, but still... As it turns out, God was there too. We saw some beautiful things we wouldn't have seen if we had spent the day riding to the top and looking around there.

It wasn't about where we ended up, but how we ended up. When we keep our focus on God first, we see Him wherever we are. When we focus on ourselves, well, it makes us a little short sighted. We miss the big picture because it's hard to see past ourselves.

The experience made me consider something else that has been bothering me lately. There is a popular phrase going around that says, "It ain't about me." And that is true…it ain't. It's about the kingdom of God. I know the sentiment is intended with good intentions, but it can't accomplish what it hopes to.

Maybe it is just the word nerd coming out in me and no one else would notice this, but I'm a writer, and analyzing words and the nuances of their meanings—the emotions they elicit—is what I do.

When I hear or see the phrase "it ain't about me," I think about ME. It's not possible to do otherwise.

Saying "it ain't about me" turns my attention to... me. Even if I think of all the reasons it isn't about me, I'm still thinking about me.

If you don't believe me, try it. Say the word "me" and see the first image that comes into your head. I bet it looks a lot like the person who stares back at you in the mirror every morning.

It is hard to serve others—to esteem others as better than myself as Scripture instructs—if I'm thinking about me. "Me" can have no place in my thoughts if I am truly desiring to serve others.

The result is different when I say, "It's all about God." Now, I go straight to thinking about God, which I believe is the goal of the misguided saying. "It's all about God" leads me to think about God and why it is all about Him. It leaves me out of the equation...where I belong.

And when I think about God, I think about all the things He loves.

We must be careful of things that sound good on the surface but are really counterproductive. If "it ain't about me" becomes our mantra, we'll be a bunch of well-meaning Christians running around with our attention focused on ourselves. And isn't this what the enemy longs for?

If, when we learned of the collapsed tunnel and subsequent change in our plans, we had said, "Well it ain't about me," I contend that we might have gone on to Eiger exactly as we did. But it would have been with a spirit of having to settle for something that wasn't our choice. The conversation in our heads might've sounded something like, "It isn't about me and what I want, so I'll just settle for this other thing because it is never about me or what I want or think."

Who wants to serve the Lord with that mentality? I'm pretty sure the Lord doesn't want to be served with that mentality either.

What we focus on, what we allow to capture our attention, really does matter. And if I'm honest, "ME" makes a pretty unproductive and unsatisfying topic.

Questions for Reflection:

> Try this…approach a task you don't really want to do by telling yourself, "It ain't about me," and note how you feel. Now approach the task, telling yourself, "It's all about God." How does this feel different?

> How might our acts of service become more meaningful and powerful by making this one shift in our perspective?

19

The Root of Bitterness

Make every effort to live in peace with all men and to be holy; without holiness no one will see the Lord. See to it that no one misses the grace of God and that no bitterroot grows up to cause trouble and defile many (Hebrews 12:14-15 NIV).

In Texas where I live, mesquite trees are an invasive and often destructive problem. Ranchers have been known to refer to them as devil trees or the devil with roots. They are hard to destroy.

We can cut them off at ground level. That solves the problem for about a day before they come back—with enthusiasm. The mesquite tree has a tap root that reaches deep underground. Far down the root is a knot, and in order to get rid of the tree for good, we have to dig down to that knot and cut it out. Anything less, and we'll have to deal with that tree again before too long.

Bitterness in my soul is the same. It comes in so easily—a comment made or a look given. Sometimes, it floats in like the soft, weightless seeds of the dandelion, so lightly that I don't know I've allowed an offense to settle in and turn to bitterness.

But once it takes root and starts to grow, it interrupts my fellowship with God.

Less than ten seconds of watching the news tells me I'm not alone in this. The urge to be bitter is a temptation, and we know from whom temptations come. We want to give in to bitterness because it is our justification for feeling anything other than love toward another.

Sometimes, we must distance ourselves from the source if we aren't yet able to withstand the temptation: social media, certain people, the news channel. As long as we feed the root of bitterness with the um…fertilizer freely available from these sources, we won't be able to dig down and remove the root.

I know some situations are impossible to avoid. Your job, your neighbors. But what if it's your church?

I suggest that until I can recognize the source and deal with it, this is when I need to step away. My tendency to be fertile ground for bitterness always stems from something in me more than anything someone has done to me. Perhaps the offense spoke into one of my insecurities or threatened the control I try to keep on my life—or highlighted the fact that I'm not really in control.

My bitterness will be contagious. Perhaps in the way I respond to a comment or answer a question, what I attend, or where I sit. A look here or there. Body language that reflects something other than joy and the peace that passes understanding. On a bad day, I might be tempted to make an innocent remark that isn't really innocent at all. Like the weightless seeds of the dandelion, I will spread bitterness. And Scripture tells me that then it will grow up to cause trouble and defile many.

Keeping myself in the same environment that feeds my bitterness only distracts me from getting to the true source. Like the pesky mesquite trees, I can be so busy fighting what is above the surface that I don't take time to dig down below and get to the real source of the problem.

Until I'm willing and committed to the effort of identifying and destroying the root of bitterness, it will continue to thrive in my soul, gradually edging out the love that wants to grow there.

Questions for Reflection:

What has bitterness caused you to miss out on? Friendships? Ministry opportunities? Peace? Contentment? Joy?

What steps can you take to eliminate the root of bitterness and overcome the damage it has done?

20

A Boy, a Bracelet, and a Belief

And this is the testimony: God has given us eternal life, and this life is in his Son. Whoever has the Son has life; whoever does not have the Son of God does not have life (1 John 5:11-12 NIV).

It was written all over his precious face. Eyes bright, smile wide, and steps eager. He believed what he offered was valuable, and we would want it. In his belief, he ran forth with confidence and the joy found only in those with a childlike faith.

And because he believed, I now own a bracelet made of cheap, black and blue beads. It cost me a dollar, but it is priceless.

When the tour buses stopped beside the rocky, barren heights overlooking the Valley of the Shadow of Death, I couldn't imagine anything joyous being found in this desolate place. Then three little boys appeared out of nowhere. It wasn't as if they could hide behind a tree and wait for people to show up. But from wherever they came, they came with zeal and arms loaded with black and blue bracelets.

They were Bedouin children from one of the ramshackle camps nearby. I suspect the only English they knew was "one dollar," the price of a bracelet. They were irresistible in the way they darted from one potential client to another, always smiling even when the answer they received was no. And there were lots of wrists adorned with cheap, beaded bracelets when the buses pulled away.

I didn't need a bracelet, but I paid their price for the blessing of joining in their joy.

It shouldn't have surprised me when God turned a bracelet into a lesson for my heart.

Do I share the gospel with as much enthusiasm as these boys selling strings of beads?

Does the joy on my face make people want what I have?

Do I persist, undaunted by rejection, confident in knowing if not this one, then another?

I know God wasn't asking me these questions because my answer was yes—it wasn't. He asked me these questions to reveal my heart to me, to teach me, and to help me see how a follower of Christ should look and act.

We have something to share far more valuable than a string of glass beads. Yet often we share with reluctance, with fear and self-doubt, looking as if we're uncomfortable to bring it up. Are we afraid we might offend someone with the good news? There will be those who are determined to take offense. So pray, smile, and move on.

But there's a flip side to our eagerness—a shadow mission to our ministry. These are the times when we run forward with eagerness, but we share the wrong things.

You should come hear our new pastor—he's really cool. Our praise band is phenomenal. You should see the cool new technology, decorations, smoke machine... We mention everything but the power of the gospel at work in our church.

We sell a Christianity to wear on our wrist instead of one that changes our hearts.

The problem doesn't lie in these people using their talents in the church. Those are talents given by God to use for the glory of His kingdom.

The problem lies in when we, as members of the body, start believing this is what we have to offer the lost. When we offer anything less than—or other than—the gospel, thinking that is enough. Making our church relevant to the people we are trying to reach might not be wrong, but there is danger when we make how relevant our church is the object of our worship.

When it feels easier to sell people on entertainment than on eternity, we may be tempted to offer the cheap beads of the world when what we really have is the priceless treasure of eternity.

Questions for Reflection:

What do you wish others truly knew about God? How can you share this with them?

What are the things you allow to fill your worship, and are they drawing you closer to the heart of God?

Walking in the Reign

Loving Ourselves

Walking in the Reign

21

Puzzled No More

*Now you are the body of Christ, and each one of you is a part of it
(1 Corinthians 12:27 NIV).*

Winter puzzle season. In early November, the jigsaw puzzles make their appearances. With great confidence and enthusiasm, we clear off a spare table, dump out the pile of pieces, and begin working the tiny fragments together in gleeful harmony until we have a beautiful picture.

That is the vision, anyway.

This year we added a new one to our collection. A one-thousand-piece picture of the Swiss Alps at sunset. Since only three colors were needed to print it, they could afford to sell it at a discounted rate. A little black along the bottom edge where the landscape is in shadows, shades of orange as the sun bounces off the mountains, and blue sky. At least one half of this puzzle is nothing but amoeba-shaped tidbits of blue cardboard. And this is why my husband no longer has the privilege of deciding which puzzles to purchase. But we were able to use the money we saved for the marriage counseling needed afterwards.

Now, because I'm a problem solver—or maybe because I am impatient and easily frustrated—I often try coaxing a piece of the puzzle into the place I need it to go. But we all know what happens when I do this—anything less than a perfect fit throws off the entire puzzle. The piece made to go there now must find another place where it wasn't really meant to be and so on and so forth.

I believe God appreciates a good puzzle too. He designed each of us—all our curves and edges—to fit exactly where He needs us in the bigger picture. I admire the artistry and creativity that goes into making the mosaics of faces using tiny tiles of other faces. I think this might be how God sees humanity.

Every person has a specific place he or she fits. When they aren't in place, it leaves a hole. When they try to fill a place that isn't theirs, it throws the picture off.

The world tries to shove us into places we aren't intended to be, jamming our hearts into a hole too small, too tight and confining, bending and battering us until it looks like we fit. Or a hole too big for us, too much open space around us, leaving too much room to wiggle until we're broken.

The world doesn't care about the bigger picture of God's creation. It seeks to serve its own needs by telling us we should go here, be on this committee, serve this ministry, stay in this job and sign our kids up for XYZ.

But, when we find the place we were uniquely designed to fit, everything clicks. We cease to struggle against our inner nature, trying to fit a role not meant for us. A piece of God's puzzle in the perfect and proper place, filling the role only it can fill in order to make the mosaic of God's kingdom the magnificent masterpiece He intended.

Sometimes, it's not easy to find the place we are meant to be. I often pick up pieces of the puzzle that are close fits. They look like they might be the one, only to find that isn't their place after all. Sometimes we need to try different things before we find our perfect fit. Sometimes, learning where we don't fit is part of discovering where we do.

Questions for Reflection:

When are the times you feel you are in the place you were meant to be? What are the things that make you feel unfitted or out of place?

In which do you experience the most peace? How can this awareness help guide your choices?

22

What Does "Living Your Best Life" Mean?

(by Emily Dehm)

"Whoever wants to be my disciple must deny themselves and take up their cross and follow me. For whoever wants to save their life will lose it, but whoever loses their life for me and the gospel will save it. What good is it for someone to gain the whole world, yet forfeit their soul?" (Mark 8:34-36 NIV).

Like most of you reading this, I'm sure you have come across the "Are you living your best life?" posts on social media. If you are anything like me, your scrolling finger hesitated for a second as you pondered what seemed like a simple question. It caused your mind to wonder.

You may have lifted your eyes from the screen temporarily, looking around you, trying to pinpoint what exactly your life even was. You may have glimpsed the dirty dishes in the sink, miles of city and interstate instead of trees and nature around you, the basket of laundry poking out of the bedroom. Your brain desperately searched for an answer among the mess. This wasn't the life you signed up for, and you have no idea how to bridge the gap between what you envisioned and a harsher reality.

Alas, you have no good answer for this Facebook post, so you continued aimlessly scrolling. It would be easier if you just didn't address it, just slid on past it. Out of sight, out of mind.

I want to break this question down a little.

You see, in recent weeks, I have pondered the deeper side of this question. I mostly see it in reference to jobs and career paths, comparing eight-to-five positions to work-from-home, but I have also been aware of it in respect to self-care methods, shopping, houses, relationships, and so forth.

The life you live isn't directly defined by your career or how often you get your nails done. I don't think those are terms you can base "your best life" on. In the grand, elaborate scheme of things, we are just tiny, little specks. It isn't about us or our unceasing enjoyment of life. We selfishly seek what we think will grant us the highest yield of happiness.

I think truly living your best life is a constant effort. I'm not going to wake up tomorrow morning and say, "This is my best life."

The moment I say that, I feel I will have grown complacent. I will become stagnant in my actions, my choices.

Living your best life is the pursuit of Jesus instead of money, the acceptance of Jesus' agenda instead of your own, dedicating quiet time to spend with Him, learning from Him, and being thankful in all situations.

Living your best life can potentially be enhanced by the blessings around you, but they do not actually define your life. Your best life is how you are choosing to pursue God and demonstrate His love to those around you.

When you arrive at the pearly gates, God isn't going to ask if you lived your best life. He will ask if you used the talents, the circumstances, the gifts He gave you to glorify Him.

In glorifying God, you live your best life. Your best life is not self-promotion.

If I'm being honest, I am not always happy with where my life is right now. I long for a cabin tucked on a mountainside with wildlife and beautiful skies around me. I wish I had way more time to spend with my husband than I do. I want to read books for a living and never return to my gray cubicle of an office. Luckily for me, I can choose to glorify God no matter where my life is. Glorification of Him is not contingent on my circumstances.

So today, look at the question in a different light, with a fresh perspective. Are you truly living your best life?

Questions for Reflection:

Do you find yourself promoting yourself and your plans, displacing God's design for your life?

Take a look at your current season and circumstances. Are you seeking to glorify God in each aspect of the good and the bad?

23

Facing Our Fears by Looking Up

For God has not given us a spirit of fear, but of power and of love and of a sound mind (2 Timothy 1:7 NKJV).

Acrophobia, the fear of heights. And the curse of a woman whose husband and offspring are seemingly fearless.

They get a mutual enjoyment out of tormenting me by dangling themselves from high places.

But I've found it is good to challenge myself by facing some of my fears. When I do, I often experience something I would have otherwise missed, and I allow God to grow my faith.

That's why, a couple of years ago I found myself on the entirely too wobbly and far too tall platform for a zip line at a women's retreat. I didn't want to do this, and I was sure God would still love me even if I backed out. But ever since I'd registered for the event, knowing it was a completely optional activity, I had the unmistakable feeling this was something I was supposed to do. I felt God was extending an invitation to experience something new. I waited until the last minute, praying the feeling would pass. But God kept whispering in my ear, "Do you trust me?"

With great angst—the kind that is just short of wailing and gnashing of teeth—I harnessed up, climbed the unstable steps, sat, and yes… scooted myself inch by inch to the edge. I know my legs completely freeze up when my fear kicks in, so there was no way I could step off the platform like all the fearless people were doing.

It wasn't a pretty launch, but I managed to lean forward enough to let gravity do what I couldn't. I won't lie—the instant I left the platform was nothing short of sheer terror. But in the next moment, I was flying and free. And I was aware that as I kept looking up to God, the distance between me and the ground no longer scared me. For a few moments, I was swept away in a moment of surrender to the Lord. *Yes, Lord, I trust you.*

God had not given me the fear of heights, but He would use it to teach me.

Recently, I did something else that scared me—a helicopter tour of the island of Kauai. I'd never flown in a helicopter before, and I am not a fan of flying (the acrophobia thing again). But I knew my husband wanted to go, and that he wouldn't if I didn't. So being the Proverbs 31 wife that I am, here I went again.

And it was spectacular. I saw parts of the island I never would have been able to see if hadn't done this. Beautiful, breathtaking scenes that could only have been created by the unfathomable creativity of the Master Creator. Things that could only be seen from a sky view.

We can't avoid every disease, accident, or loss of a loved one. Whether we want to or not, we will face things that scare us. I believe God gives us opportunities to stretch our faith to teach us to trust Him. For me it has been zip lining and helicopter rides. Taking a risk is an opportunity to build our faith muscles. By trusting God in facing some of these fears, we learn to trust Him in facing those we don't get to choose.

Facing the things that frighten us, we step off the edge and let go, falling into the loving arms of our Father. Then He can bring us to places of victory we couldn't have imagined.

All it takes is faith as small as a mustard seed when you take that first step. Or in my case, that first scoot.

Questions for Reflection:

> What situations are you facing right now that God may be using to grow your faith?

> How big is your faith? How big would it feel if you faced a difficult situation? How might facing this fear grow your faith?

24

Out of the Tomb

Then Jesus said, "Did I not tell you that if you believe, you will see the glory of God?" (John11:40 NIV).

How would we respond to seeing Lazarus emerge from the tomb? I had never considered what my response would have been until a friend stated that if she'd been there, the passage in John 11 would have said, "When he had said this, Jesus called in a loud voice, 'Lazarus, come out!' The dead man came out, his hands and feet wrapped with strips of linen, and a cloth around his face...and Julie ran."

I laughed at her comment, but if I'm being honest, my response might have been the same as hers. What it must have been like to stand among the mourners and watch as Lazarus, dressed in his raggedy grave clothes, came staggering out of the grave he'd been in for four days like a man just getting up from a four-day nap.

But how about the other side of that? When I have to let go of someone, let them slide into the cold, distant darkness of the tomb, so that Jesus can do what He needs to do with them? The tomb of sinful living, the tomb of disobedience to God, the tomb of pride or greed. Even the tomb of unbelief.

As Christians, we never want to turn our backs on someone who needs our help. That isn't Jesus' plan for salvation at all.

But when those people become anchors that threaten to drag us into the shadows as we try to reach into the darkness and save them, we need to know that is not God's will for us. There will be times when we may have to let a loved one go into the grave of their choosing. Thankfully, we can do so trusting that even when we must let go, God never does.

Cutting ties is not the same as abandoning them.

Martha allowed Lazarus to be placed in the tomb, but she continued to cry out to Jesus in faith. And it is important to know she did it from outside the tomb. She didn't need to go into the tomb to be heard. Martha remained in the light praying, not sitting in the dark keeping the dead company while waiting to see what would happen.

She couldn't hold her brother back from the tomb. The smell of death and decay would have started to wreak havoc on her life, covering her in the same stench of hopelessness. Martha knew when it was time to let go.

Like Martha, sometimes we must turn loose of people who are dear to us so that Jesus can do what He needs to do. And so the smell of death doesn't infiltrate our lives, ushering us to a grave of our own. A grave of sorrow, depression, hopelessness, anger, bitterness, hurt—the list is long, but the remedy is the same for all.

Once we have given someone to God, we will be free to step into the light and pray for them in righteousness. The Bible then tells us the prayers of the righteous are powerful and effective (see James 5:16).

If we hold on to things in our lives that keep us from walking in a manner worthy of the gospel—even if by doing so we hope to pull another from the darkness—we cannot be righteous in our prayers. And sooner or later, the smell of death and decay will start clinging to us as well.

It's not easy. And it is certainly not painless. There are people in my life that I have or am still going through this with. Don't think I've never had the thoughts that *if I had just prayed harder or sooner or better, Jesus would have come, and my Lazarus would not have had to go to the grave.*

But Jesus tells me to have faith, to trust, to believe.

"Then Jesus said, 'Did I not tell you that if you believe, you will see the glory of God?'" (John 11:40 NIV).

Lazarus had to be allowed to go to the grave before Jesus could do what He needed to do with him.

And so those who beheld—that includes you and me—might see the glory of God and believe.

Questions for Reflection:

What are the "graves" that have threatened to pull you or someone you love into the darkness? Have there been times when attempting to help someone else has put your own faith in jeopardy? How might the story of Lazarus help you pray for others?

When have you seen the redemptive glory of God in the transformed life of someone who was lost?

25

The Lion Monument

Put on the full armor of God, so that you can take your stand against the devil's schemes (Ephesians 6:11 NIV).

Mark Twain referred to the massive stone carving in Lucerne, known as the Lion Monument, as "the saddest and most moving piece of rock I have ever seen."

From the moment it comes into view, there is something gripping and poignant about the dying lion carved in the sandstone side of a former rock quarry. Even before I knew the story, the expression of grief—a mixture of pain and sadness and regret—on the lion's face resonated deep within my heart.

The inscription above the lion translates, "To the Loyalty and Bravery of the Swiss."

Curious to know exactly how they inspired not just such a moving monument but such an honor on the inscription, I did some research once I returned home.

There was a time in Swiss history when the upper class generated their income streams by enlisting young men as mercenaries for hire to other countries. This is how nearly one thousand of these mercenaries, known as the Swiss Guard, came to protect the French monarchy of King Louis XVI at the time of the French Revolution.

On August 10, 1792, with approximately seven hundred soldiers stationed at the royal Tuileries Palace, a mob of angry citizens numbering in the thousands overtook the castle. The king, feeling the fight was hopeless, sent a note to the Swiss Guards ordering them to lay down their weapons. The King, whether out of fear and desperation or poor judgment, believed the rioting crowd might be placated by the action. He issued an order that was, in essence, a death sentence to those men. The soldiers, knowing what fate awaited them if they complied, ignored the King's order, continuing to fight until their ammunition gave out.

The carving of the dying lion shows a wooden stake driven through his heart, and it also shows his paw lying protectively over the shield bearing the fleur-de-lis of the French royalty.

The history behind this monument fascinates, moves and inspires me. But I couldn't help but also recognize our battle for God's kingdom in it as well.

Would loyalty and bravery be noted on an inscription about my life? I certainly hope I live in such a way that it would.

What I do know is that my King will never tell me to take off my armor or lay down my weapons. Not when I'm sitting in church. Not when I'm teaching vacation Bible school. Not even when I'm in the midst of praise and worship at a Mercy Me concert. Never.

Our enemy does not quit. He is no respecter of battle lines or boundaries. And our King knows this.

Sure, the enemy may allow me periods of peace where I can get comfortable and overconfident to convince myself there is no battle being fought. That's the trap he uses to catch me without my armor.

Flash forward from the massacre of the Swiss Guards only a few decades later, and we find ourselves at the battle of the Alamo. When Santa Anna came to San Antonio in preparation for the siege of this small mission, he rode in under a black flag. It meant no quarter. Even to surrender was certain death.

Satan, too, rides under a black flag—the flag of no quarter. The flag of certain death.

The Apostle Paul tells us in his letter to the Ephesians, *"Therefore put on the full armor of God, so that when the day of evil comes, you may be able to stand your ground, and after you have done everything, to stand" (Ephesians 6:13 NIV).*

I haven't yet found the verse that tells me to take it off this side of eternity.

Questions for Reflection:

In what ways can you sense the urgency of a battle going on around you? Are there places you go where you are tempted to lower your guard?

Reread the description of the armor of God in Ephesians 6:11-18. How can you apply each of these things to a situation you are dealing with in your life today?

26

Planting Seeds and Pulling Weeds
(by Emily Dehm)

"The kingdom of heaven is like a man who sowed good seed in his field. But while everyone was sleeping, the enemy came and sowed weeds among the wheat, and went away. When the wheat sprouted and formed heads, then the weeds also appeared" (Matthew 13:24-26 NIV).

One of my favorite things about reading the parables of Jesus is that I get a new message from them each time. As I read this morning, God revealed a beautiful analogy to me.

Our lives are like the wheat field. We have planted our "good seed," and it's growing. We see it beginning to sprout and do very well, but we grow lax in cultivating it. It seems to be doing well on its own, so we lessen our care.

And then the enemy, who senses our lessened attention, comes to sow ugly weeds into our once fruitful harvests.

This spoke very heavily to me this morning. I don't know about you, but I am someone who slacks off on cultivating my fields. Not intentionally, of course, but sometimes I feel busy or tired or think "there'll be plenty of time for that tomorrow."

Do you grow weary of constantly watching over your life's crops? Do you grow relaxed and read less of God's word, immerse yourself less in His love?

Do you allow the enemy to sneak in and sow his weeds in your once beautiful wheat field?

Do you even know there are weeds?

When we stop paying close attention to our lives, thoughts, words, and hearts, we allow the enemy to come in and do what he does best…steal, kill, and destroy. We let him sow a weed or two, and before we know it, our lives are a jungle of weeds and calloused hearts.

As a kid, I used to mow the yard at my dad's office. I always dreaded it. The mowing wasn't as bad as pulling the weeds and stickers. The weeds always seemed so deeply rooted, and it took forever to get them all out of the yard and flower beds. (No joke…sometimes I thought I might pull up a root that was a mile long.)

Because that's what weeds do. They take root when we aren't paying attention, and they grow and prosper. Before you know it, you are desperately tugging to uproot them in hopes of restoring your flower beds.

The enemy does the same in our lives. He has no problem sowing all the weeds in the world into our crops.

As Christians, we must remain vigilant against the enemy. Dig into God's word, pray, and allow God to protect your crops. Weeds are sneaky...not there when you go to bed, but there when you arise. And speaking from experience, they so totally grow back with a vengeance.

Consider your crops. Do you see weeds rearing their ugly heads among your wheat?

Identify your "weeds" and get busy pulling. Cultivate your life, sow God's word and truth, and send the enemy his eviction notice, effective immediately!

Questions for Reflection:

> What are the "weeds" Satan wants to sow into your life? Do you allow your heart to be fertile ground for these "weeds"?

> What circumstances tempt you to neglect tending to your "crops"? How can you guard against this?

27

Posers

But he said to me, "My grace is sufficient for you, for my power is made perfect in weakness." Therefore I will boast all the more gladly about my weaknesses, so that Christ's power may rest on me (2 Corinthians 12:9 NIV).

It turned out to be great entertainment sitting outside the Coliseum in Rome watching other tourists pose for pictures in front of this iconic piece of history. Gone are the days when you simply smiled and tried not to blink. We saw every kind stance, head tilt, arm placement, knee and hip angle you could imagine—and I won't even get started on the lip puckers. Some of our favorites were the "joy jumping" poses. These people would spend forever repeatedly jumping until the unlucky friend with the smart phone captured just the right moment.

It was exhausting just watching. I'm sorry, but having my picture made shouldn't be a cardio event.

I did wonder, though, if they had any concept of the historical treasure in the background. Whatever they thought of it, they were determined to capture a moment that looked like they were overcome by joy from the experience. Posing instead of just being.

Satan loves posers. He even gets excited when he can just convince us we are posers. If Satan can't make us doubt God, he'll try to make us doubt ourselves.

And it goes something like this...

We surrender something—our life to the Lord or maybe our right to hold a grudge—and Satan whispers in our ear that we didn't really mean it. He wants us to doubt our sincerity or our motives because by doing so he can get us to question our salvation.

After all, if we had truly accepted Christ, we wouldn't still struggle with the thoughts in our heads or the desires of our flesh, right? Fear, doubt, jealousy, and pride would be non-issues if I truly meant what I said when gave it to Jesus, right?

It doesn't take much work on the enemy's part, and pretty soon we're hearing our own voices say, *"If I really loved God, I wouldn't have those thoughts. I wouldn't cringe when I hear that woman's voice. I wouldn't be tempted to..."* You fill in the blank. You know the areas where the enemy comes for you.

The Apostle Paul confessed that *"...I was given a thorn in my flesh, a messenger of Satan, to torment me" (2 Corinthians 12:7 NIV).* Paul doesn't say what this thorn was or how it tormented him, and there is all sorts of speculation. But I don't think it was an issue of physical pain. Paul's body had endured so much physical abuse, I can't imagine him not being in almost constant pain or discomfort. And he certainly wouldn't have referred to it as a mere thorn in his flesh. I think there may have been something deeper, something that touched his soul. Did he have regrets he couldn't let go of? Did he have doubts about his purpose or his worthiness?

Was this the same thing that prompted him to confess, *"I do not understand what I do. For what I want to do I do not do, but what I hate I do" (Romans 7:15 NIV)?*

We don't know, but we can take comfort in knowing Paul, who as Saul had an extremely intimate encounter with Jesus on the road to Damascus, still struggled with something that Satan had access to and attempted to use to his advantage.

In the passage from Second Corinthians, Paul goes on to say that he had pleaded with the Lord three times to take it away: *"But he said to me, 'My grace is sufficient for you, for my power is made perfect in weakness'"(2 Corinthians 12:9 NIV).*

What God never says is that we must be perfect, never make a mistake, or have a doubt. He says, *"My grace is sufficient for you."*

There are a lot of things I can pose as in this life—a gifted homemaker, erudite author, or the infamous Proverbs 31 woman. But if I have accepted Jesus Christ as my Lord and Savior, I can never pose as a Christian. I may be tempted to pose as a flawless Christian who never questions or doubts or fails to love my neighbors. Being a perfect Christian who has it all together is a pose.

Being a faulty, sometimes wayward, imperfect Christian is the real deal. And I have peace in knowing the gap between my imperfections and the glorious perfection of God is filled with my Lord and Savior, Jesus Christ. He is standing in the gap for me every time I don't measure up.

But you will still never see me posing in the "joy jump." My insurance deductible is too high.

Questions for Reflection:

What do you struggle with that makes you feel unworthy?

What things might you attempt if you believed God's grace was sufficient for your weaknesses?

28

Rock Flour

For God, who said, "Let light shine out of darkness," made his light shine in our hearts to give us the light of knowledge of the glory of God in the face of Christ (2 Corinthians 4:6 NIV).

Rock flour. Contrary to what my family may say, this is not an ingredient in my homemade biscuits.

Rock flour is, however, the substance that gives glacier-fed rivers and lakes their incredible color. Formed by the friction created as glaciers move slowly over the rocky terrain, grinding against the rocks, the material known as rock flour is so fine it doesn't sink but stays suspended in the water. To oversimplify what happens, this rock flour then reflects the green and blue light rays back for us to see, giving the water its brilliant, turquoise color.

Rocks—places of stony hardness—can build up inside our hearts.

Not kidney stones or the feeling one gets after eating my biscuits. I'm talking about the grief, betrayal, abandonment, guilt, and a list of wounds too lengthy to cite. These are things that can and will harden our hearts if we allow it.

These hardened places can become like stones, piling up until they obstruct our relationship with God and keep us from receiving the good things He has for us—love, joy, peace. Like a dam made of stones stopping a stream, they can build until they become a barrier to the ability of God's love to pour through us.

We will all face wounds of some kind in our lives. When we do, we often try to rid ourselves of that pain as quickly as possible by turning to some other emotion—bitterness or anger perhaps. It might even feel good or justified for a while. But it's only temporary relief. Left untended, the rocks will build until, finally, we have dammed the flow of God's love, and we are left with the aching absence of God's nearness. We've built a wall of stone from our hurts and left Him on the other side.

But when we give God access to those places, like a massive glacier moving over the side of the mountain, He will begin the grinding process.

Little by little, God will take the hardened places and mill them into bits and fragments that permeate who we are—our unique personalities shaped by our life experiences—without blocking the flow of good things in and through us.

The bad and painful things that have happened to us don't go away as if they never were. Forgiving and letting go isn't forgetting. Memories cannot be erased.

But God can transform them into something that loses its power to go on hurting us.

Will the process be painful? Probably so. Will it be difficult? It is a fight for your life. Will it take a long time? Only God knows. Will the result be beautiful and glorious? Absolutely.

Because once you have allowed God to do what only He can do, the real magic happens.

Then particulate matter—the rock flour of our souls—reflects the Son's light back into the world around us.

People will see something different in us, something beautiful, radiant, and breathtakingly glorious. Just like the spectacular beauty of those glacier-fed lakes.

I had the opportunity to witness this at a funeral recently. God had taken nearly thirty years to grind the lifetime of hurts, the feelings of abandonment, the lies, and memories too painful to share into a substance that radiated His glory as a family came together again. Where anger and unforgiveness could have spread a black cloud over the day, grace and mercy reflected the Son's light to everyone who came. What started as a funeral for a reclusive relative few had seen in years turned into a celebration of love and reconnection. It was a beautiful example of what God can do when we give Him permission to start grinding.

Questions for Reflection:

What wounds in your past may have been allowed to turn to places of hardness?

How would it feel to be free of those places?

29

Simple

The Lord preserves the simple... (Psalm 116:6 NKJV).

Webster's dictionary tells me something considered to be simple is not hard to understand or do, not fancy, not special or unusual.

The reality, though, is that simple has gotten hard to understand, almost impossible to do, and most definitely unusual. The world we live in is no longer simple, and sometimes, it seems like the idea of simplicity frightens us, as though we've become convinced that if something is simple, it isn't good enough. Accepting something that is simple is settling for less than we deserve.

The opposite of simple is difficult, hard, demanding, complicated, complex, fancy, or elaborate. Which one of those words appeals to you most? Which one of those sounds compatible with a life filled with joy and happiness? All I hear in that list of words is stress, exhaustion, failure, and depression.

When did being simple become a crime? Simple is not the same as lazy or complacent. It is not even a sign of a lack of ambition. I believe it is a sign of refusing to be sucked under by the popular opinion that more is still never enough.

"The Lord preserves the simple…" (Psalm 116:6 NKJV).

This use of the word "simple" refers to those who are innocent, clean, untarnished. *Untarnished?* In this world? Is that even possible? It's a challenge at best, an impossibility if we don't fight for it.

And that is where simplicity comes in.

Simple doesn't start with our calendars, agendas, smart phones, or even our minds. It starts with our hearts. Knowing what truly brings us joy, what our hearts were really created to love, each one as unique as our individual fingerprints. Our hearts are created to love and worship God through the unique passions and gifting He has given each of us.

When I think of simple, I'm reminded of an experience my husband had on an old pipe rail in front of the local post office. It was the middle of a Texas summer day—hot. Coming out of the building in the middle of his workday, he met an old friend he hadn't seen in a while—a retired gentleman who didn't get out as often as he used to.

Gone are the days when there might have been a bench out front, so they sat on the low pipe rail fence in front of the building and talked.

It was a simple visit, and yet the conversation was far more important than they realized. In their simple moment, they were unaware they were being watched. An older woman came out of the post office, and with tears in her eyes, told them how much it touched her to witness their visit. It took her back to the days as a child when people did such things.

Such things? Such things as knowing their schedules weren't too full to simply stop right where they were to sit and talk about whatever it is men talk about sitting on the pipe rail in front of the post office as the world speeds by.

It didn't require a smart phone or an app. Just a simple pipe rail in front of a building and two hearts that understood the gift of the moment.

Simple. Sacred. Satisfying.

I've had a heart check lately contemplating how much of what I do I do because, well…that's the way it's done. Everyone else is doing it. It's expected.

But do I truly care if my house looks like a professional decorated it? Do I really want to spend hours in the kitchen preparing a gourmet meal when something less complicated could be just as satisfying? And the biggest, maybe hardest question: Do I really feel I live an inadequate life if my schedule isn't jam-packed and color-coded down to the minute?

What if I could regain my ability to live with simplicity? Would I be happier? Would I appreciate my life more if I filled it with less? Would I enjoy the people in my life more? Would I walk in step with the Holy Spirit better?

A simple life is born in the heart when we understand what gives us joy, fills us with peace, and brings us into the presence of the Lord. You know what these things are for you. They may have been buried under the color-coded calendar and mountains of to-do lists, but somewhere in your heart, you remember.

Simple. Sacred. Satisfying.

Questions for Reflection:

> What areas of your life would you enjoy more if they seemed less complicated? What can you let go of or change to make that happen?

> What are the things from your past that draw you back to something simpler? What stands in the way of enjoying those things again?

30

A Portion and Path

LORD, you alone are my portion and my cup; you make my lot secure. The boundary lines have fallen for me in pleasant places; surely I have a delightful inheritance (Psalm 16:5-6 NIV).

In preparation for this trip, I had been careful with my health, exercising regularly, taking vitamins, and staying rested. (Okay, I always do the rested part.) It wasn't cold and flu season, but I didn't want to take any chances on my trip to Israel.

My months' worth of healthy living seemed pointless when the fever and sore throat set in during our five-hour layover in New York. I don't think I have ever had a cold manifest itself as quickly or aggressively as this one did. By the time we boarded the plane for the next leg of our trip, I had my carry-on full of overpriced pharmaceuticals from an airport vendor—and no small amount of frustration.

This might be a once-in-a-lifetime trip, and I wasn't planning to miss a moment of it. I wanted the full experience. And I somewhat self-centeredly wanted to feel good while doing it.

The weather was hot in parts of Israel, and we were on the go from sunup to sundown. About halfway through the trip, I crawled into bed after an exhausting day, unsure if I'd be able to participate the next day. The cold had turned into a sinus infection, and I was miserable.

Now, I don't believe God made me sick any more than I believe it was the work of Satan. But both would use it to their advantage if I allowed. Who I allowed in was my choice.

There is always a blessing to be had if we look closely enough, so I inquired of the Lord what He had for me in this (that's how they would have said it in the Bible, anyway). As Jesus often does, He answered my question with a question. What I heard was, "Is this enough? Am I enough?"

Jesus asked me if what I had was enough. Would I choose to be grateful, or would I choose to complain? I was in Jerusalem. I was walking in the Holy Land. I had made it through several days touring places in Galilee. I had a busload—literally—of new friends whom I'd shared sacred moments with. Was experiencing the Sea of Galilee enough if I couldn't make it to the Temple Mount?

Would I be grateful for what I did have? Or would I look to what I might not get to have and complain?

More importantly, if I'd never been able to visit Israel, was Jesus alone enough for me?

I recalled a time when I had prayed for God to help me recognize, respect, and accept with joy the portion and path He had for me in life. There are things I will never do because they haven't been given to me to do. The level of peace I experience in my life will reflect how willing I am to embrace the portion and path I have been given, rather than coveting the portion or path given to another.

Can the clay question what the potter makes of it (see Romans 9:21)?

David wasn't allowed by God to build His temple, but he prepared the way and readied the materials so that his son Solomon could. David accepted God's plan and didn't try to move ahead without Him (see 2 Samuel 7). He was neither resentful nor complaining. He was obedient. And *"God testified concerning him: 'I have found David son of Jesse, a man after my own heart; he will do everything I want him to do'" (Act 13:22 NIV).*

Or there is the parable of Jesus concerning the talents (see Matthew 25). The servants who had been obedient with what they were given were invited to *"Enter into the joy of your Lord" (Matthew 25:23 NKJV).*

The invitation wasn't based on how much they achieved or produced but is for those who had been obedient.

I have friends who are Christian writers—some are multi-published, some are just published, and some are *please, Lord, let me be published*. They all feel called to write, but each of their journeys is different. Some are prolific, making books appear at regular intervals throughout the year. Some take years just to get the first draft on paper. How long does it take to write a book? It takes as long as God says it takes.

It goes without saying that a good work ethic is required. Without a work ethic, failure is on the horizon. But there is a peace to be found in obedience.

The delays and obstacles, the setbacks and missteps, can be confusing and discouraging. That's when I remind myself God is the One who gives me my portion and path. He gives me just the number of words I need for that day. I may have to row my boat out on the Sea of Galilee and cast my net to catch them—that's the work ethic—but they are a gift from Him. He gives me the ideas I need to pursue, and He times the giving so as not to overwhelm me, but to draw me closer to Him.

And I'll have just enough days to write the portion of words He gives me.

I want to see my book completed. No one ever starts a project they hope they never finish. But God knows exactly how far I'll get with the portion and path of life He has given me. He is already aware of the end and has the next step in place. My job is to be obedient to His direction in all that I do. It is, after all, more important to have my name written in the Lamb's Book of Life than on the bestseller list or whatever worldly goal or pursuit we're after.

The amount and quality of peace I experience depends on how willing I am to embrace my portion and path. This is true whether I'm writing a book, saying goodbye to a loved one, or tucking myself into a strange bed half the world away from my home and wondering what tomorrow will bring—and where to find the nearest pharmacy.

Can we, like David, be content with our portion and path?

Questions for Reflection:

> Do you see your place in life as a gift from God to be grateful for or a struggle you must deal with?

> Do you believe God has a portion and path specifically planned for you? Are you willing to accept that portion and path in obedience to God?

 Lori Altebaumer is a wandering soul with a home keeping heart. Now that her nest is empty, she enjoys traveling with her husband and visiting her adult children where she can rummage through their refrigerators and food pantries while complaining there's nothing good to eat there.

 Emily is a frequent blogger who writes about navigating through life as a young adult and a child of God. She loves the Lord above all else, but then her husband, reading, and mountain air. Not always in the same order.